T0383474

The Five Lives of
Hilma af Klint

THE FIVE LIVES OF

HILMA AF KLINT

PHILIPP DEINES

David Zwirner Books

I. The Search Begins

Hilma af Klint was forty-four years old when she turned her life upside down and abandoned academic painting, her trained profession. But in fact, Hilma's search for new forms and ideas began much earlier, in her teenage years.

Gustaf af Klint (1858–1927)
Hilma's brother was the eldest af Klint child. What became of him? He joined the Swedish Navy and became an officer, like the men of past generations of the family.

Hilma af Klint (1862–1944)
The heroine of this story, Hilma reinvented painting. There were no models to inspire her abstract works, only the benevolent spirits that stood by her side. They encouraged her to take a path nobody had walked before.

Ida af Klint (1860–1938)
Hilma's older sister was two years her senior. She fought for the rights of women and was a member of an organization that championed women's suffrage. She also worked in a museum, got married, and started a family.

Hermina af Klint (1870–1880)
Not even a photo remains of Hilma's beloved little sister. She died suddenly, at a young age, shortly before Hilma's eighteenth birthday. The artist struggled with her sister's death throughout her life.

Victor af Klint (1822–1898)
Hilma's father was the reason Hilma was born in a barracks. At the time, Victor af Klint headed the military academy at Karlsberg Palace, near Stockholm, and lived there with his family for several years. He had liberal ideas and saw to it that his daughters Ida and Hilma were well educated.

Mathilda af Klint (1830–1920)
Hilma's mother's family originated in Finland and belonged to the local Swedish minority. In her old age Mathilda went blind, so Hilma lived with her and took care of her.

Stockholm on a Sunday morning in 1879.

Storkyrkan, in Stockholm's old city

6

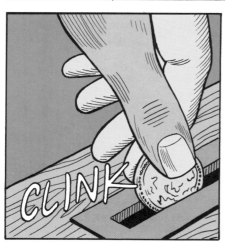

Saint George and the Dragon, Bernt Notke

Vädersolstavlan (*The Sun Dog Painting*), Jacob Elbfas, Urban målare

Bertha Valerius regularly hosted séances at Gripsholm Castle.

She would become Hilma's mentor.

During the séances, the circle would try to contact the invisible world.

Driven by an involuntary force, the participants went into a trance and drew the messages they received from the spirit world.

KRRR

They spoke in tongues.

Everything was meticulously recorded.

They conversed with the dead.

Sometimes it got a bit spooky.

Voltaire's friendly spirit appeared.

The botanist Carl Linnaeus called himself a translator of plants.

A spirit named Charles spoke of a future art period:

We will need nothing more than the delicate waves that surround us like air. Painting shines the light that artists create in their own minds.

And:

To create a work of genius, artists harness the pure force of pure intent, beautiful and free from earthly defects.

From Gripsholm Castle to Stockholm, it's about thirty-seven miles by boat.

Hermina?

Yes.
I'll always be
by your side.

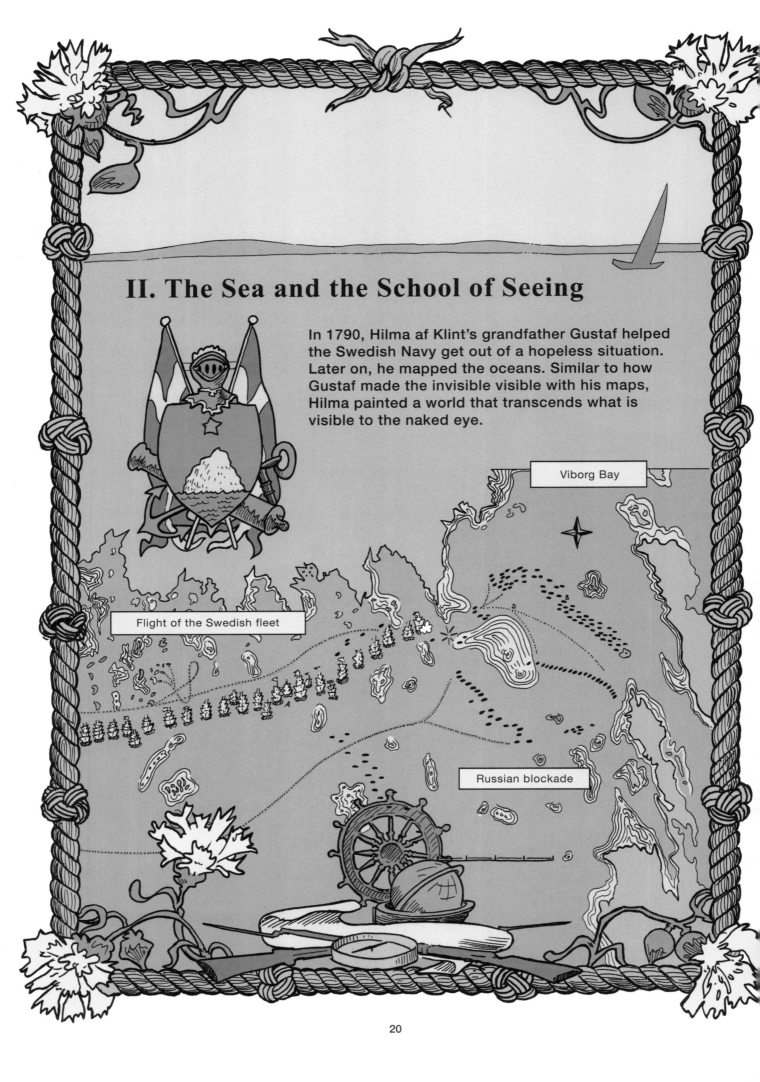

II. The Sea and the School of Seeing

In 1790, Hilma af Klint's grandfather Gustaf helped the Swedish Navy get out of a hopeless situation. Later on, he mapped the oceans. Similar to how Gustaf made the invisible visible with his maps, Hilma painted a world that transcends what is visible to the naked eye.

Viborg Bay

Flight of the Swedish fleet

Russian blockade

Fredrik Klint (age 14)   Erik Klint (age 57)   Jonas Klint (age 11)   Gustaf Klint (age 19)

King Gustav III had gone to war on the *Amphion*. The state vessel was completely inadequate for battles at sea.

Your Majesty, the sloop is ready.

King Gustav III of Sweden

Admiral! The king is coming aboard.

22

The greater part of the Swedish fleet escaped the Russian blockade on that summer day in 1790. Shortly thereafter, King Gustav III made peace with Russia.

Just two years later, he was murdered at a masquerade ball.

Verdi's opera *A Masked Ball* was inspired by this event.

His son Gustav IV was crowned King of Sweden at the tender age of thirteen.

His uncle Karl would serve as his guardian until he came of age. In 1809, he was forced to abdicate after a coup d'état. Karl, the admiral of the fleet, then had himself crowned king.

King Karl XIII of Sweden

Erik Klint was ennobled in 1805. From then on, the family was allowed to use the name "af Klint" ("of Klint") and hold a coat of arms. The af Klints were also given two small country estates on the island of Adelsö.

Gustaf mapped the oceans. The famous Swedish sea atlas is his work.

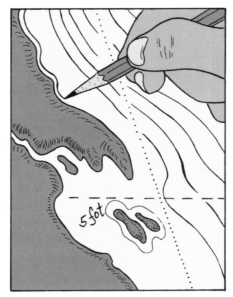

5 fot

SWERIGES SJÖATLAS

Gustaf af Klint

In 1825, he became the vice admiral of the Swedish Navy.

Vice Admiral Gustaf af Klint

Unfortunately, Hilma never met her grandfather. Still, he was important to her. She drew his portrait and hung it in her studio.

Like her grandfather, Hilma wanted to make the invisible visible. Her paintings can also be read like maps.

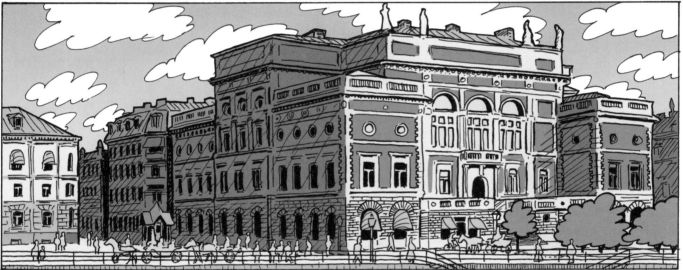

Royal Academy of Fine Arts, Stockholm

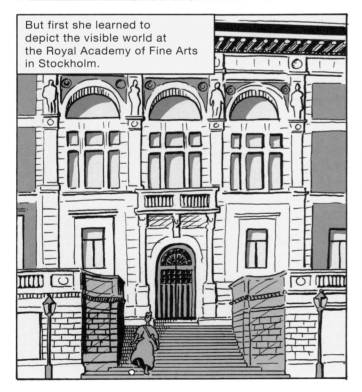

But first she learned to depict the visible world at the Royal Academy of Fine Arts in Stockholm.

Hilma took up her art studies in 1882. Women had been allowed to study at the Royal Academy of Fine Arts in Stockholm since 1864, but the young men and women were instructed separately.

1. Carl Larsson, 1889   2. Otto Weininger, 1903   3. August Strindberg, c. 1900   4. Paul Julius Möbius, 1902   5. Alfred Dührssen, 1900

Still, Hilma and her female classmates learned a great deal at the Academy.

Anatomy

Drawing nudes

Clothed women drawing nude men

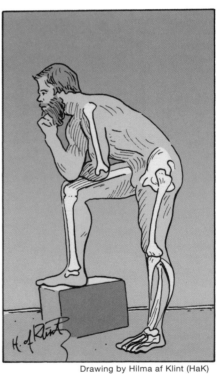

Drawing by Hilma af Klint (HaK)

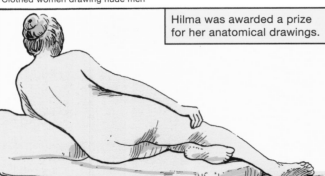

Hilma was awarded a prize for her anatomical drawings.

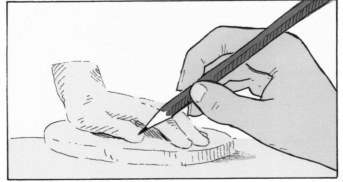

HaK

HaK

32

Hilma developed a keen eye for the visible world. She mastered the art of drawing and painting it.

HaK

Portraits

HaK

Landscapes

HaK

HaK

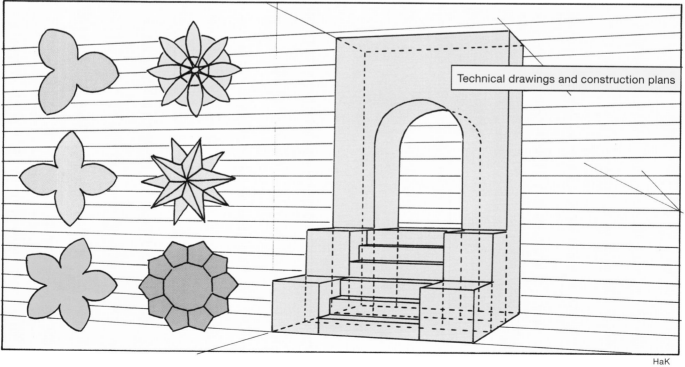

Technical drawings and construction plans

HaK

33

Gustave Doré

Émile Bin

Frederic Leighton

For her rendering of Andromeda, Hilma received an award from the Academy. Her work is very different from the interpretations by famous male painters.

Not a monster!

Not a hero!

No fear!

HaK

...

The Academy's studios were in the Atelier Building on 5 Hamngatan, in the heart of Stockholm. This is where Hilma exhibited most frequently.

After her studies, she made a name for herself as a landscape painter.

Blanch's Café, a meeting place for Stockholm artists, was near her studio. Hilma met her friends there for tea.

Aside from painting, she also illustrated children's books.

HaK

HaK

Blanch's Art Gallery often put on group exhibitions that Hilma participated in.

HaK

HaK

HaK

HaK

She received commissions for portraits and painted local cityscapes and landscapes.

HaK

HaK

HaK

To earn money, Hilma and her friend Anna Cassel worked at the Veterinary Institute in Stockholm.

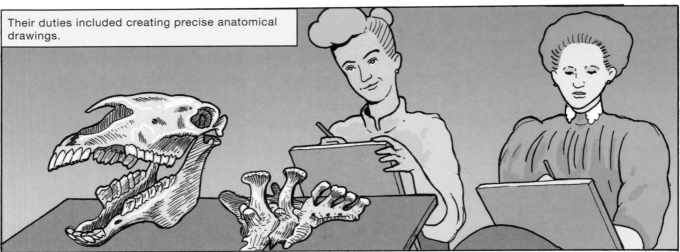

Their duties included creating precise anatomical drawings.

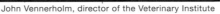
John Vennerholm, director of the Veterinary Institute

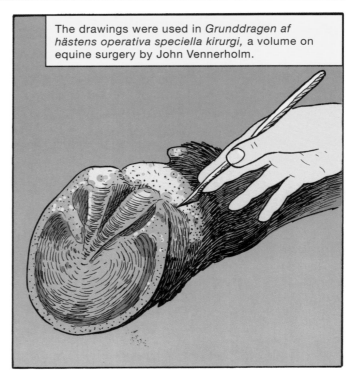

The drawings were used in *Grunddragen af hästens operativa speciella kirurgi,* a volume on equine surgery by John Vennerholm.

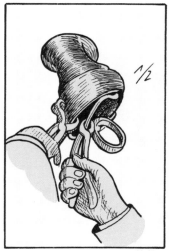

HaK

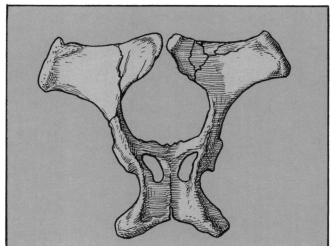

HaK

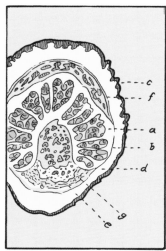

HaK

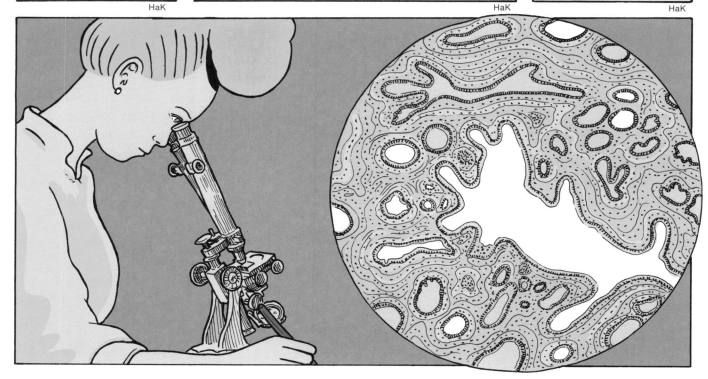

Whenever Hilma could, she spent time in nature.

She would sit still in a tranquil spot and take note of what she saw and felt.

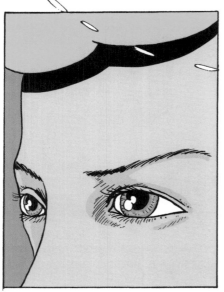

She developed her own profound way of seeing.

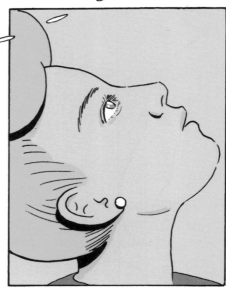

Willenskraft und Demut

Willpower and humility

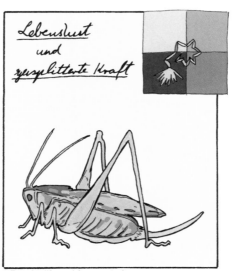

Lebenslust und zersplitterte Kraft

Zest for life and fragmented power

Erreichte Fähigkeit den Geschmacksinn zu beherrschen

Mastering the ability to channel her sense of taste

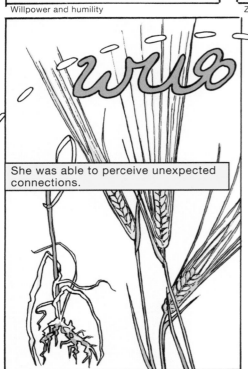

She was able to perceive unexpected connections.

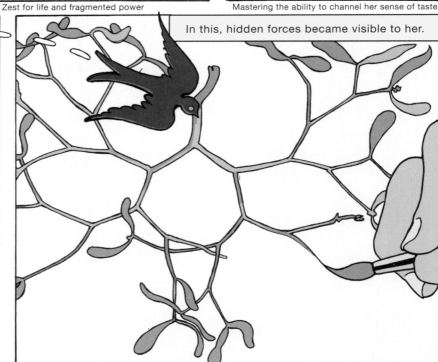

In this, hidden forces became visible to her.

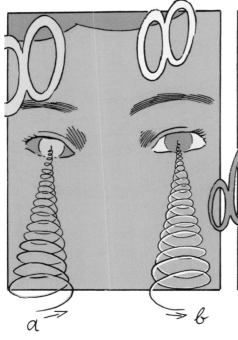

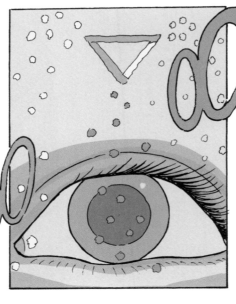

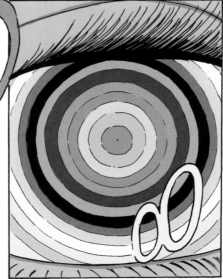

III. The Path to Abstraction

For Hilma af Klint, nonrepresentational painting was the natural expression of the forces that hold everything together. Her paintings were meant to open doors to new feelings and thoughts.

Green represents the connection between the two sexes.

Blue represents ♀.

Yellow represents ♂.

Sperm

Snails (bisexual animals)

Purple represents overcoming dualities.

Vestalasket signifies the connection between Hilma and Anna.

Mathilda Nilsson

Cornelia Cederberg

Sigrid Hedman

Anna Cassel

Hilma af Klint

The group known as "The Five" met regularly to pray, meditate, and sing together.

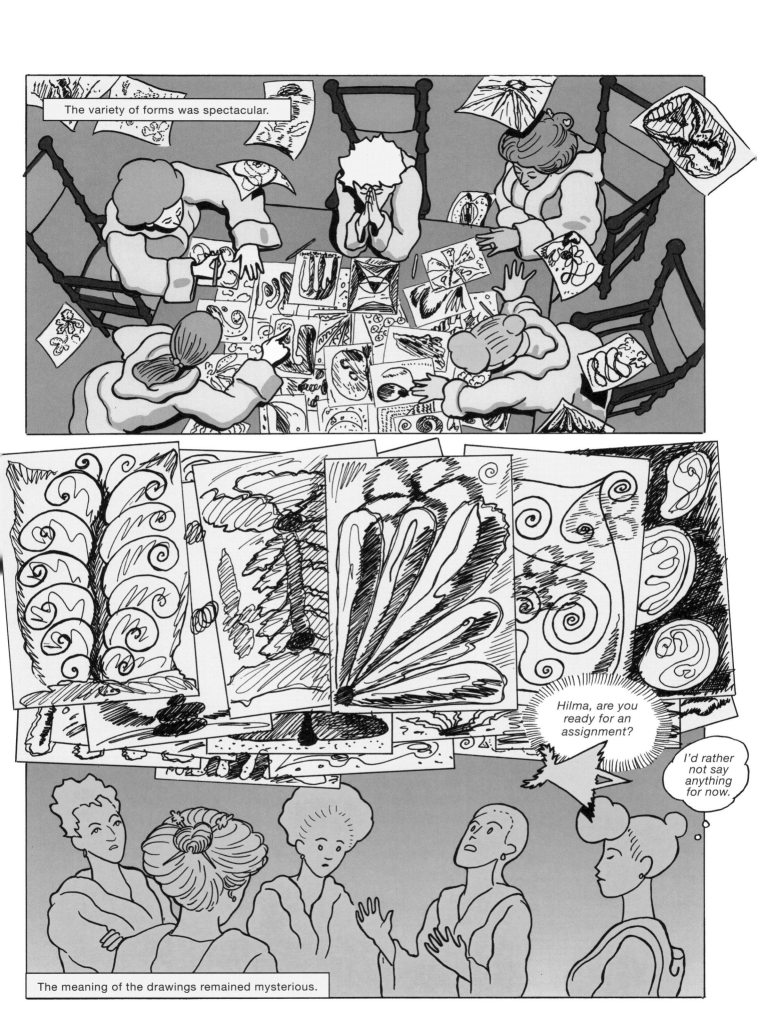

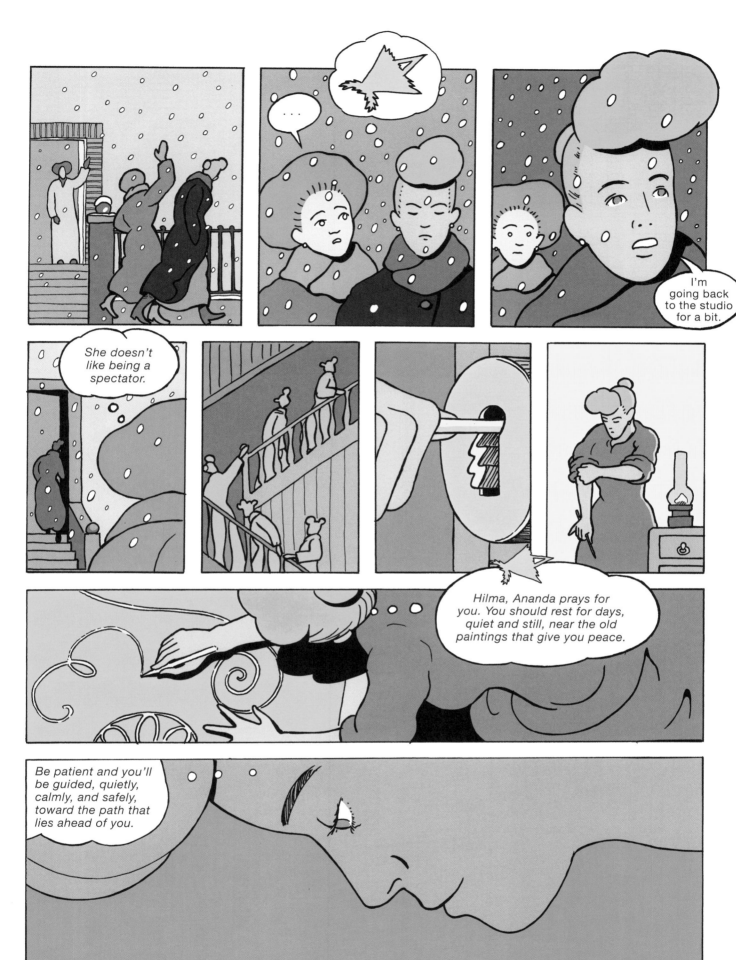

In 1903, Hilma and Anna embarked on a great journey. The first leg took them from Stockholm to Trelleborg.

I didn't want to say anything in front of the Five, but the spirits speak to me directly.

The others aren't going to like that!

Saint Nicholas Church, Trelleborg

50

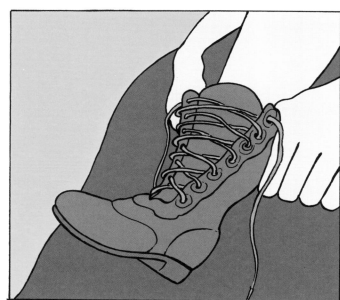

Morning in Trelleborg Harbor.

There was regular ferry service between Trelleborg and Sassnitz on the island of Rügen.

I am so small, so insignificant, but I feel such tremendous power flowing through me. It's pushing me forward.

Sassnitz Harbor, Rügen, Germany

From Sassnitz, the friends took the train to Berlin.

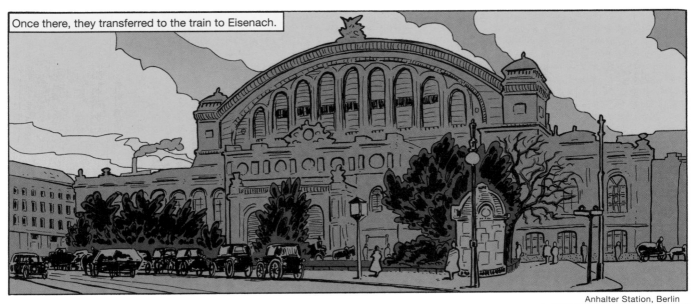

Once there, they transferred to the train to Eisenach.

Anhalter Station, Berlin

They visited Wartburg Castle.

This is where Martin Luther went into hiding.

This is where he prayed and worked.

Saint George!

The artists continued their journey southward. Their route took them through the Alps.

Milan was their first stop in Italy.

Duomo of Milan

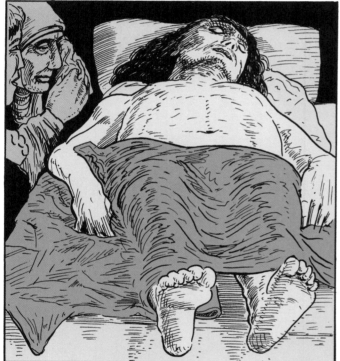

Lamentation Over the Dead Christ, Andrea Mantegna

The Kiss, Francesco Hayez

The Last Supper, Leonardo da Vinci

57

Verona

How beautiful!

Piazza delle Erbe

Madonna and Child, Giovanni Bellini

The Holy Family, Andrea Mantegna

And tomorrow, Venice!

Venice

Grand Canal

The descent of the spirit into matter . . .

. . . the ascent of matter through the spirit.

Eternal Father, Ludovico Mazzolino

59

The Uffizi and Palazzo Vecchio

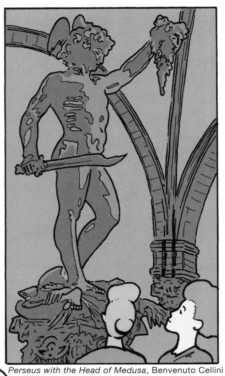

Perseus with the Head of Medusa, Benvenuto Cellini

Madonna Enthroned, Giotto di Bondone

I would love to make large paintings!

Cathedral of Santa Maria del Fiore   Palazzo Vecchio

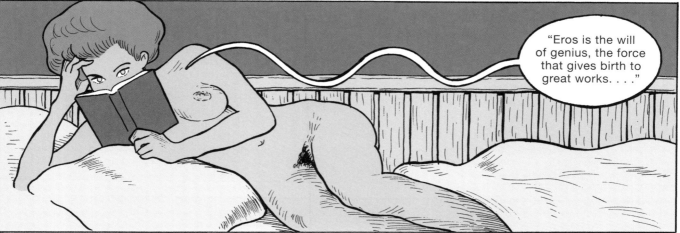

"Eros is the will of genius, the force that gives birth to great works. . . ."

The Secret Doctrine, Helena P. Blavatsky

Basilica di San Lorenzo

61

Saint Peter's Basilica

Saint Peter's Square

Pietà, Michelangelo

The Colosseum

Roma Termini Station

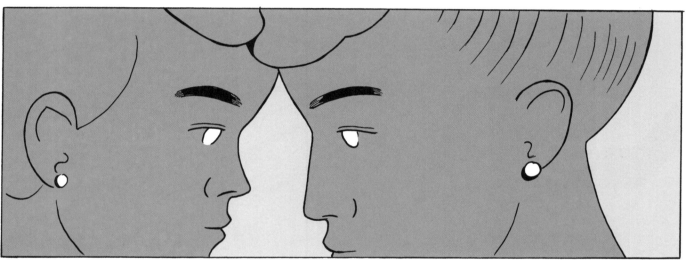

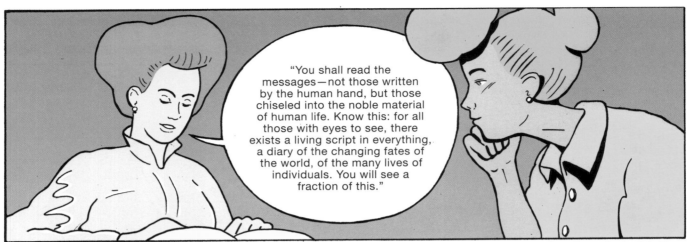

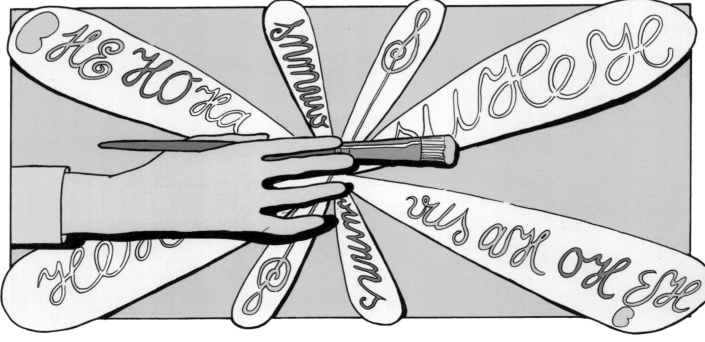

From one of Hilma af Klint's notebooks

Knowledge of life lies hidden in the knowledge of human duality, in the law of completion.

From one of Hilma af Klint's notebooks

From one of Hilma af Klint's notebooks

71

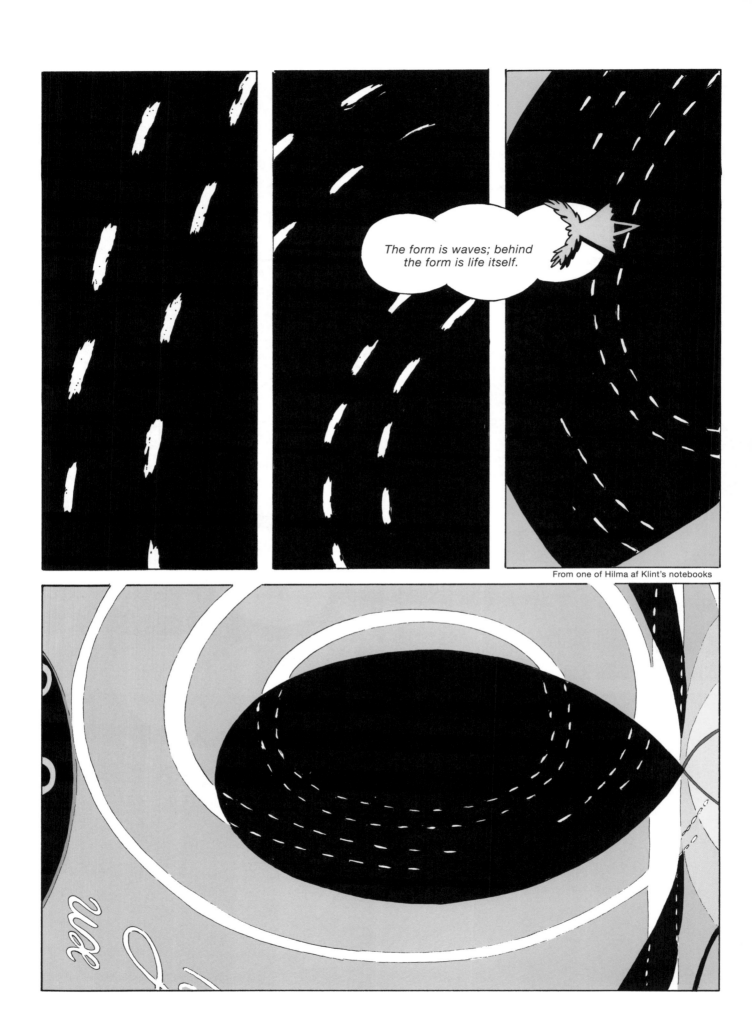

From one of Hilma af Klint's notebooks

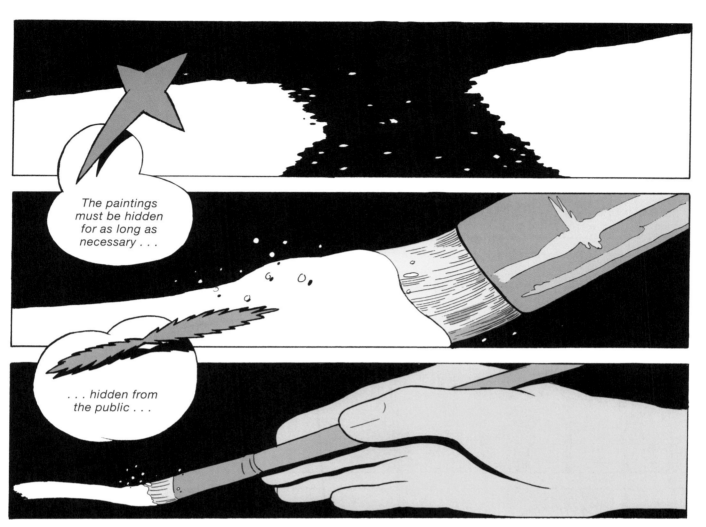

From one of Hilma af Klint's notebooks

The way artists in Stockholm, Paris, or Berlin understood art at the beginning of the twentieth century was entirely different from what Hilma af Klint was painting.

Anders Zorn (1860–1920)

Carl Larsson (1853–1919)

Richard Bergh (1858–1919)

Ernst Josephson (1851–1906)

Georg von Rosen (1843–1923)

Edvard Munch (1863–1944)

Piet Mondrian (1872–1944)

The most famous artists in Sweden and the rest of Europe were all men.

Pablo Picasso (1881–1973)

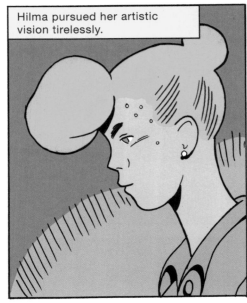

Hilma pursued her artistic vision tirelessly.

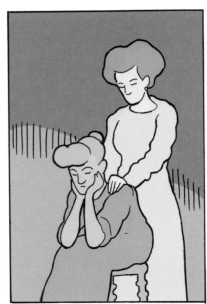

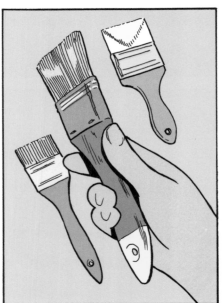

The paintings were painted through me . . .

From one of Hilma af Klint's notebooks

78

From one of Hilma af Klint's notebooks

IV. The Suitcase Museum

Hilma af Klint's paintings were literally overwhelming: many were so large that it was difficult to transport them. People who wanted to see them had to come to Hilma's studio. But around 1920, the artist had a brilliant idea. She designed a suitcase museum. It contained two miniature versions of each work—a colorful watercolor and a black-and-white photograph. She glued these images into ten albums and took them with her when she traveled.

Rudolf Steiner, the founder of anthroposophy, repeatedly visited Stockholm to lecture in front of large audiences.

Steiner's sun seal

Steiner's Saturn seal

Rudolf Steiner (1861–1925)

Steiner's moon seal

Royal Swedish Academy of Sciences

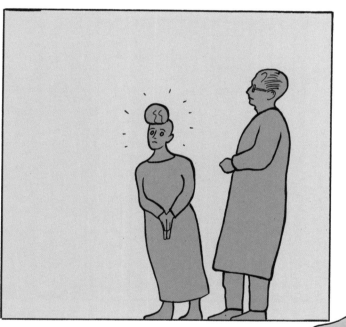

87

Forget Anna!

We're a couple now.

Hilma spent most summers on Munsö, a large island in Lake Mälar, near Stockholm.

Tomorrow, I'll show you the island.

From one of Hilma af Klint's notebooks

From one of Hilma af Klint's notebooks

From one of Hilma af Klint's notebooks

A flower's soul is not attached to a body, which is why humans can experience it.

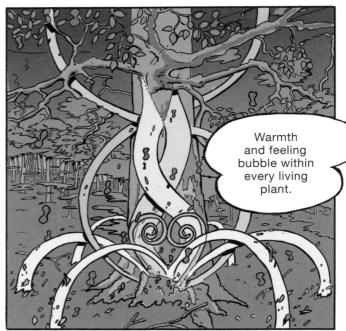

Warmth and feeling bubble within every living plant.

From one of Hilma af Klint's notebooks

Platonic solids

Pierre and Marie Curie

Thomasine shared her extensive scientific knowledge with Hilma.

1. Atomic structure of radium, Niels Bohr

2. From *Art Forms in Nature*, Ernst Haeckel

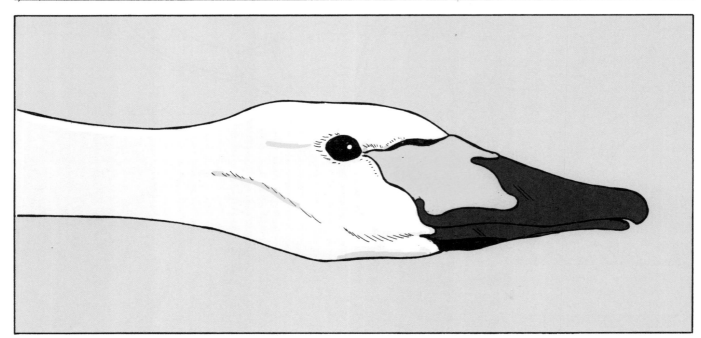

In 1914, the First World War broke out. Hilma remained in Sweden, while Thomasine worked as a nurse for the Red Cross on a hospital ship.

In 1918, the war finally came to an end.

The war destroyed plants and killed animals, leaving behind empty spaces that could be filled with new forms, if only there was enough faith in the human imagination and human capacity for creating higher forms.

From one of Hilma af Klint's notebooks

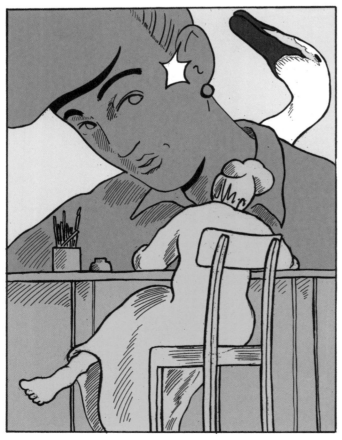

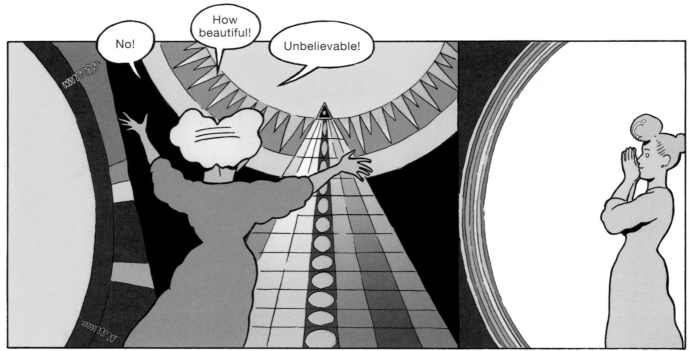

Group X, No. 3, Altarpiece

Group X, No. 1, Altarpiece

Group IX/UW, No. 14, The Dove

Group IX/SUW, No. 17, The Swan

Group IV, The Ten Largest, No. 2, Childhood

Group IV, The Ten Largest, No. 4, Youth

Group IV, The Ten Largest, No. 7, Adulthood

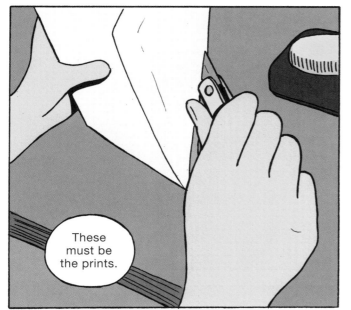

101

Basel

Grüezi, Frau Andersson. Grüezi, Frau af Klint.

We can go listen to Dr. Steiner first thing tomorrow.

I'll talk to him right after the lecture.

Starting in 1920, Hilma and Thomasine repeatedly traveled to Dornach in Switzerland. There the anthroposophists had created a place to live, work, and study in a community setting.

Sometimes the two stayed for several months, sometimes for just a few weeks.

The Goetheanum was rebuilt—this time in concrete.

Hilma was able to win over at least one admirer in Dornach.

Peggy Kloppers-Moltzer

Rudolf Steiner didn't live to see the new building—he died in 1925. Hilma and Thomasine visited Dornach for the last time in 1930.

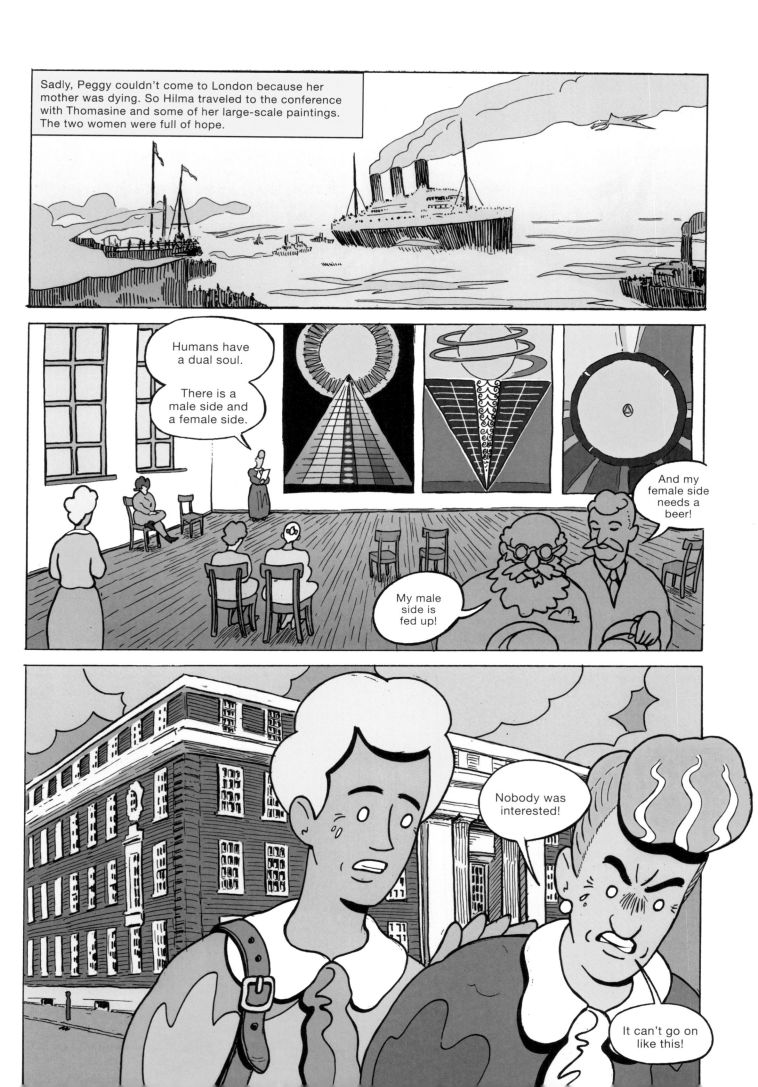

V. The Temple

After exhibiting her paintings in London, Hilma af Klint had to admit to herself that her art always evoked the same reactions in her contemporaries: Resistance. Indifference. Arrogance. She came to the conclusion that the time for her paintings hadn't yet come. Her art would only be understood in the future. For Hilma, this insight was not an end but a new beginning. With the help of her friends, she began to put her estate in order. She burned some of her notebooks while others were copied.

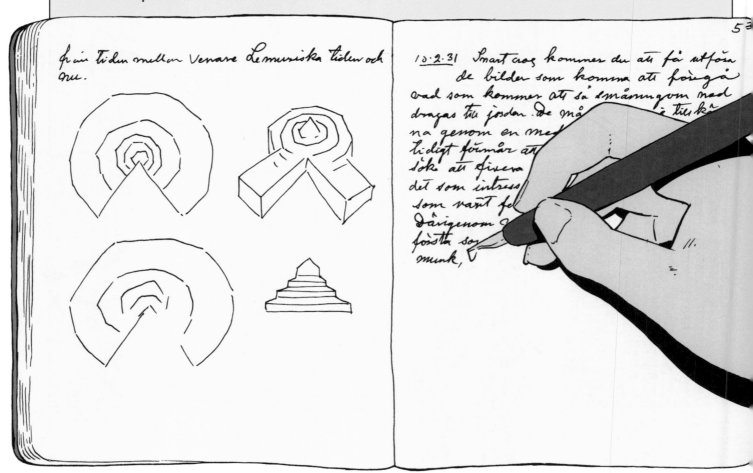

Thomasine and Anna helped sort and revise the materials.

Many notebooks had to be marked with "+×" signs.
They could not be shown until twenty years after Hilma's death.

In 1930, when the artist was almost seventy years old, the familiar voices returned. They asked whether she wanted to accept a commission. At first, Hilma hesitated. But then she agreed.

In the weeks that followed, she designed a temple for the future. Visitors would traverse the building in a spiral. She wanted to store all 193 of her *Paintings for the Temple* there.

In 2018, the Solomon R. Guggenheim Museum in New York opened a major retrospective of Hilma af Klint's work. The exhibition became the most visited in the history of the museum. And just as she had wished, Hilma's paintings hung in a spiral.

AFTERWORD
JULIA VOSS

In 2008, I saw one of Hilma af Klint's paintings for the first time.

I was still an editor at the *Frankfurter Allgemeine Zeitung* and had traveled to Stockholm to write about an exhibition at the Moderna Museet. When I entered the room where painting no. 17 from *The Swan* series was hanging, my heart started beating faster.

"What is this painting?" I asked Iris Müller-Westermann, the curator of the Moderna Museet, who was giving me the tour.
"This is Hilma af Klint," she said, and reported what she knew about the artist: This hitherto little-known Swedish woman studied painting at the Royal Academy of Fine Arts in Stockholm. At the age of forty-four, she turned her life upside down and embarked on a path of painting in ever more innovative styles. Her estate comprised over one thousand paintings, many of them abstract. The earliest of her nonrepresentational works originated in 1906.

I was stunned. In equal measure, I was happy and furious. On the one hand, I was pleased to have discovered this unusual work, which I sensed was so much more than simply a good painting. On the other, I was angry to have found yet another female artist who had been passed over by art historians. I had studied art history, written a dissertation in the field, and been working as an art critic for several years. How could it be that I did not even know her name!

Since then, I have been preoccupied by two questions: Why did Hilma af Klint paint in the manner she did? And why has she remained unknown for so long, and not only to me? In 2013, Müller-Westermann curated the fantastic exhibition *Hilma af Klint: A Pioneer of Abstraction* at the Moderna Museet, which traveled to the Hamburger Bahnhof — Museum für Gegenwart, Berlin. I then published an article in the *Frankfurter Allgemeine Zeitung*, "Art History Needs to Be Rewritten." I earned praise and criticism from museums, art historians, art critics, and my own editorial department. Several of my colleagues shared my enthusiasm, while others feared we might risk our good reputation. Many vociferous voices did not want to see Hilma af Klint in the canon of abstraction.

In 2017, I decided to leave my job at the newspaper, learn Swedish, and write a biography of this extraordinary woman. To my family, this decision did not come as a surprise. Both of my children could say "Hilma af Klint" before they even learned about Pablo Picasso or Leonardo da Vinci. During summer vacations, we now traveled north rather than south. In Sweden, Johan af Klint, Hilma af Klint's grandnephew, showed us the places where his grandaunt had lived. Johan took me to Hilma af Klint's archive. He invited my family to his country house. His wife, Christina, took us mushroom foraging in the woods and made us the best sandwiches we have ever eaten. When Johan took the children canoeing on a crystal-clear lake, our sons learned an important lesson: in Sweden, swimming weather is much less frequent than it was at our previous holiday destinations in the south. But the water is so clean everywhere; it invites you to simply jump in. To this day, we are all in awe of the beauty of the Swedish countryside.

My husband, Philipp, and I started to have a special kind of conversation. In the spring, when I decided to write Hilma af Klint's biography, we flew to Florence together. In the artist's archive, I had discovered a thin notebook with the title "Italian Trip." Underneath one of the drawings, she had written "Florence." We hoped to find the exact spot where she had made the sketch. Finally, Philipp discovered the hotel window that still offers an almost unchanged view of the Basilica di San Lorenzo. When a hotel employee let us into the room, we were both very moved. Hilma af Klint had stood exactly on this spot with a pencil in her hand.

From this moment on, we wanted to know the exact details. Did she sit on the windowsill? Where did she go to eat? How did she travel? Philipp started to draw: Hilma af Klint in the hotel. Hilma af Klint at the train station. On the train. Inside the studio. Or by the sea, on the cliff that gave her family its name. "Klint" is an ancient Swedish word for "cliff." In translation, her name means "Hilma of the cliff."

The more Philipp drew, the less isolated Hilma af Klint appeared to us. In the meantime, I researched the artist to discover the previously unknown details of her life. Hilma af Klint loved to travel and did so frequently: to Italy, Germany, the Netherlands, Great Britain, and Switzerland.

Contrary to claims that she had kept her spiritual works secret during her lifetime, she had in fact exhibited them. She kept address books filled with names. She lived and worked with her woman friends, some she loved—even romantically. There were periods of ecstasy. Hearts were broken. Throughout her life, Hilma af Klint cultivated a dialogue with spirits who supplied her with messages and visions. But at the same time, she had both feet firmly planted on the ground. Her universe had room for more than just one life.

The idea for this graphic novel emerged from conversations I had with my husband, Philipp.

Someone who imagines Hilma af Klint's life as a series of drawings has different options than the author of an art-historical biography. While drawing offers greater freedom, at the same time, the imagination must operate in very concrete ways. What was the public reaction to Hilma af Klint's 1928 London exhibition? What did she think of the art on display at the Goetheanum in Dornach, Switzerland? What happened at the séances that, as her nephew Erik af Klint reports, she attended as a teenager and later?

Philipp and I frequently discussed our ideas about the world that Hilma af Klint created and the world in which she was an active participant.

In the meantime, Hilma af Klint's reputation was gaining traction. In the fall of 2018, the Solomon R. Guggenheim Museum in New York showed the outstanding exhibition *Hilma af Klint: Paintings for the Future.* It became a blockbuster, the most-attended exhibition in the history of the museum. Hilma af Klint the outsider became a star. I wrote an essay for the catalogue. In 2020, my biography, *Hilma af Klint*: *Die Menschheit in Erstaunen versetzen,* was published by S. Fischer Verlag. The English translation will be published by University of Chicago Press in the fall of 2022.

When I went out to do research in libraries or archives, Philipp sat at his drawing table. Sometimes in passing, I saw something new taking shape: The harbor from which Hilma af Klint was to begin her journey. The steamer she boarded. The ocean she crossed. On days such as these, I could barely wait to return home. I wanted to accompany Hilma af Klint on her entire journey.

The joy I felt upon seeing the finished drawings is something I hope all the readers of this graphic novel will share.

The Five Lives of Hilma af Klint
Philipp Deines

Published by
David Zwirner Books
529 West 20th Street, 2nd Floor
New York, New York 10011
+1 212 727 2070
davidzwirnerbooks.com

Managing Director: Doro Globus
Editorial Director: Lucas Zwirner
Sales and Distribution Manager: Molly Stein
Publishing Assistant: Joey Young

Project Editor: Jessica Palinski
Proofreader: Chandra Wohleber
Production: Thomas Lemaître
Printer: Livonia Print, Riga

Typefaces: Helvetica Neue, Times New Roman
Paper: Munken Lynx Rough, 120 gsm

Publication © 2022 David Zwirner Books
Text and illustrations © 2022 Philipp Deines
Afterword © 2022 Julia Voss

Originally published as *Die 5 Leben der Hilma
af Klint* in German in 2022 by
Hatje Cantz, Berlin

Special thanks to
Editorial Manager: Lena Kiessler, Hatje Cantz
Project Manager: Valerie Hortolani, Hatje Cantz

Translation of the original German text by
Renata Stein and Ruth Bittorf, courtesy
Eriksen Translations

Distributed in the United States
and Canada by
Simon & Schuster, Inc.
1230 Avenue of the Americas
New York, New York 10020
simonandschuster.com

Distributed outside the United States
and Canada by
Thames & Hudson, Ltd.
181A High Holborn
London WC1V 7QX
thamesandhudson.com

ISBN 978-1-64423-069-5
Library of Congress Control Number:
2022902692

Printed in Latvia

PHILIPP DEINES is an illustrator and artist.
He has run an independent art space and now
creates posters for techno clubs. His fashion
designs incorporate prints and patterns based
on his drawings. He exhibits his work in an
artistic context. This is his first graphic novel.

JULIA VOSS is an honorary professor at
Leuphana University Lüneburg. She studied
art history, modern German literature, and
philosophy in Berlin and London. She is an art
critic, curator, and journalist, and was formerly
the deputy head of the arts section of the
Frankfurter Allgemeine Zeitung.

Philipp and Julia are married and live with their
children in Berlin.

Philipp is grateful to the city of Berlin for its
support of this project as part of a Comic
Scholarship. Thanks are also due to the
German Comics Association (Deutscher
Comicverein) and especially Stefan Neuhaus,
for his tireless dedication to furthering the
comic genre.